FLEX WITH A PLEX

What Do People Think About Joe Mendoza?

"Joe is a big thinker, committed to learning new things every day. He is intelligent, outgoing, personable, a contributor, and a hard working individual." - Thach Nguyen

"Joe is an excellent Real Estate agent. He worked with us to find our first home and was attentive, courteous and extremely professional from the very beginning. He took time to listen to our needs and gave us ample options for us to make a decision on. He was truly a no hassle agent in that there was no pressure to make an offer until we felt it was the right fit, and his knowledge of the market conditions allowed us to obtain a great home for the price. I strongly recommend him and will use him if I'm in need of a Real Estate agent again." - Antonio Galvan

"Joe is an absolute professional whose constant objective is to provide the very best service possible for his clients. He is always looking for improvement with everything he does, both professionally and personally. As a matter of fact, we were both members of a commercial real estate program aimed toward improving one's skills. I would highly recommend doing business with him as your aid!" - Mark LaPoint

"I've known Joe Mendoza for several years. You won't find a person with a higher degree of integrity or a stronger work ethic. In his professional capacity Joe demonstrates leadership and a solid knowledge of the Real Estate Market. I give Joe Mendoza my highest recommendations." - Michael Francisco

"So, we were selling my home and at the same time we

were looking for another home to move into. And he had to go through and put in a whole bunch of bids to different homes. Every time we'd email him and say 'Hey, can you look at this?' or 'Can you look at this?' he was just patient, all over it. Going through and putting in the bids, talking to us about what his recommendations were, what he thought, and then he just really went above and beyond with that whole experience. He made it like a very seamless experience for us. He's very down-to-earth, great work ethic, and he puts the customer first."- Jeanette Ziomek

"My coach, Joe Mendoza has helped me take my business from a practice to a real business. In the last 6 months, I've taken myself out of my comfort zone, grown my team, AND my Brokerage, and looking forward to more growth. 2017 was my best year ever, and I've already set my 2018 goals to DOUBLE 2017! Let's go!!!" - Geoff Zahler

"Joe Mendoza has provided excellent real estate services to many of my friends, relatives and clients. Joe spends many hours working with the needs of his clients and is always available to find their dream homes. Joe is a wealth of information and a professional." - Melyn Acasio

"I am very new to coaching but in the last 4 months Joe has helped me transform my mindset and has kept me laser focused on exponential growth in my business. 4 months ago, real estate was just a profession for me but now Joe has shifted my mindset to a business owner. Joe is very knowledgeable, supportive, and responsive and he is exactly what I need to push me and my business to the levels I know I can achieve. Thanks Joe!" - TJ Almodovar

"He's been a high school friend so he's been our go-to person whether we're selling or buying and we've been through several of those. He's always been my husband and I's go-to person. We don't look anywhere else, he's our realtor. He is always there the moment I text or call him. The response time is amazing. I don't have to wait five minutes and he's calling me back. He's always above and beyond. There's never a time I'm waiting for him. Joe is very reliable and he will do anything and everything for his clients." - Marle Phommasy

"Joe is a great business leader, entrepreneur, and public speaker. It has been exciting to watch his real estate company grow. You won't find a more driven team to help with your next purchase. I also appreciate his persistence to get the job done. I highly recommend him." - Marla Morrison

"He helped sell one of our homes and was able to sell it quickly, and we're very happy with that result. He's a pleasure to work with and he has been in the business for quite a long time, so he knows the ins and outs." - Mei Molleman

"Joe is Awesome ! The Best! Greatest Sales Manager I ever had in 20 years in Real Estate. A proven Winner!" - David McKee

"I had the pleasure of working directly with Joe when he was coaching with Tom Ferry. Joe always has a very positive upbeat get it done attitude. He has a positive outlook on everything he decides to take on. He is a constant encouragement to all those around him with a very giving and generous spirit." - Stuart Brown

"Joe is hard working, focused and informed - a trustworthy professional." - Andrew Warburton

"I met Joe about 15 years ago. He was living in the same

area as we were and I met him, he told me he was in the real estate business and he seemed like a very trusting individual. Well, we wanted to sell it (the house) quickly, so by the time I contacted him within two days we had the For Sale sign up. Offers started coming in, he listed very quickly. So, he moved very quickly. I would tell people he is very knowledgeable. He;s been in the business over 20 years, over 25 years I believe, but the main thing is he is very trustworthy. He's always smiling and laughing so he's a pleasure to be around as well." - Elliott Nichols

"Joe is an amazing entrepreneur. 1st class human being. Expert in the real estate industry. I highly recommend him." - Pete Sanchez

"Amazing! Very focused and keeps me on track. Helped us go from 60 deals to 200 in one year." - Dustin Parker

"Coach Joe Mendoza has been fantastic! I asked for someone who could think outside the box ... He's inspiring, creative and a true asset. He's allowed me to expand my company in ways I never imagined. Thanks for everything." - David Wilson

"Joe's coaching is intuitive and on target. My business went from 9 transactions to being on track for 50 in two years. Now I have a team member, my own office space, an art gallery and am in the process of adding to my team." - Marguerite Apostolas

"The results were exactly what my wife and I expected. He was very diligent and very thorough with explaining things that we were unaware of, but most importantly he was able to prioritize exactly what we wanted so the results were beyond what we expected. We needed an inspection and he was able to be at our place for the inspection for what I believe was a duration of three hours so that right there showed us that he was dedicated to making this experience complete and stress-free for us." - Myron Mendoza

"After 12+ years in the business Coach Joe Mendoza has helped me to take my business to the next level. He is patient, knowledgeable and an absolute pleasure to work with." - Chris Remmes

"I am truly fortunate to have met Joe. He has been a real estate and business coach and most importantly a life coach. I now have a bigger vision and see the road to success and fortune much more clearly. He is always enthusiastic and on his 'A game'. He really has it in his heart to see people succeed in life." - Brian Kendrick

"He has helped me get through some tough times both in business and life. Joe is such a positive influence on my entire life, encouraging me to always perform at my best. He's taken me to the next level and given me the confidence to always reach for more." - Anthony Mosley

"Joe, would, one, actually listen when I had an issue or come up upon a situation that I haven't had before in my short term experience as a realtor and he's been a realtor for twenty years, plus. So, he listened, he understands, he also is a fantastic problem solver. He's also very motivating. He always has words of encouragement and can guide you in the right way. Through his coaching, he has given me discipline with a schedule. He's made me understand the value of offering an abundance of not only experience and information but customer care. I was previously focused on my education so I had a lot of knowledge about my area of expertise, but I didn't know how to showcase that. So, Joe helped me find my path in marketing and how to network, and how to make phone calls, scripts, what to say, that way it showcased the value in the information that I was providing clients so that I can build that long term report. It's not just a one-on-one transaction. We are trying to build relationships." - Margaret Blaisdell-Uth

"We have had such a great experience with our coach, Joe Mendoza. Not only has this coaching program given us so many great ideas to implement in our business, but the events are such a great way to meet top agents from all over the country and around the world! We have been able to grow our business 300% over each of the past two years!" - Rachel Parker

"He's my partner. Could not be where I am now without him. He is so motivating and upbeat. He has given me the direction and support I needed to take my business to the next level. With him by my side I know my business will continue to grow and crush it." - Liz Ryan

"I worked with him twice and he helped us buy a property that was for investment purposes. The last one worked out wonderfully and before that he helped us purchase a primary residence and that worked out great too. For the investment property, it was a very last minute, a quick deal, and he was available above and beyond. He made and coordinated appointments with the sellers' agent and the walk-throughs and all of that. He was available at the drop of a dime, basically, since it was such a short amount of time that we had. He was available, whenever we needed him, and was able to pull all of the parties that were involved together to get the deal done." - Cecilia Orencia

FLEX WITH A PLEX

An Introduction To Investing In Real Estate

JOE MENDOZA

FLEX WITH A PLEX

An Introduction To Investing
In Real Estate

CONTENTS

Chapter 1 Begin With The End In Mind
Chapter 2 Lifestyle
Chapter 3 K.I.S.S. - Keep It Simple Silly
Chapter 4 Just Starting Out
Chapter 5 Deeper Dives Into The Plexes - One To Four versus 5+
Chapter 6 Other Asset Classes
Chapter 7 Build A Team
Chapter 8 Deal Hunting - Visit Open Houses
Chapter 9 GIGO - Garbage In Garbage Out
Chapter 10 Be A Pain In The Ask
Chapter 11 Value Add
Chapter 12 Due Diligence
Chapter 13 Financing
Chapter 14 Rinse and Repeat - 1031
Chapter 15 Active or Passive Investing
Chapter 16 Should I Get A License Or Not?
Chapter 17 Make it a Must
Chapter 18 The Power of Focus
Chapter 19 Follow A Formula
Conclusion

Resources
About The Author

DEDICATION

This book is dedicated to my wife and kids. They hung in there with me on this rollercoaster ride and helped shape me into the person I am today. I am forever grateful.

FOREWARD

This book was written in efforts to provide great, relevant, credible information for those that are seeking to get into real estate investing, hoping to learn more, or be more inspired into action . From newbie to seasoned investors, I attempted to share some great insight drawn from personal experience and many other credible sources of wisdom in the industry. If you simply google "Joe Mendoza Real Estate", you'll see additional information and support that I've done over the last several decades, people I know, and maybe even interviewed on YouTube.

Now full disclaimer, I am not a tax, law, or financial expert or licensed professional in those industries. I would highly recommend if you do have concerns, talk to those professionals to help mitigate your risk. Remember, *competence breeds confidence*. I also do encourage you to *fail forward fast*.

Realize that you will make mistakes in the process, but the worst decision in the world is making no decision. Taking no action equals no change in your life. Are you thinking about getting into real estate and investing? Don't think too long. What sometimes saddens me is when people procrastinate way too long or they let fear get in their way. I catch up with them years later and see sometimes that they've never made any progress.

Read this book, align yourself with winners, and take mas-

JOE MENDOZA

sive action! See you at the top!

CHAPTER 1 - BEGIN WITH THE END IN MIND

When most people start this journey on investing you must definitely take massive action to make any idea you have work. I have said many times, to *learn before you earn*. However, believe it or not, there are some fallacies tied to that saying. You could read dozens of books on investing in real estate, attend real estate and investing boot camps, watch all the YouTube videos on multifamily, house hacking, etc., but if you don't ever take real action, getting out of your comfort zone, talking to absolute strangers, you'll be in the same exact place as you are today.

Some people get ready, to get ready, to never get started. They do the typical ready, aim, aim some more, and never pull that trigger and fire. Also known as *paralysis by analysis*. I'd rather you *ready, fire, aim!* Make your adjustments afterwards. If you miss, fire again, and again, and again.

Now, with that said, let's unravel a little bit about my journey.

For most of my childhood life, my dad kept saying to me, "If you want to make it in this world, you've got to be rich!" He pounded that in my head so many times. I knew in a sense that he was right because we didn't have the fancy cars, lived in a middle class neighborhood, didn't shop anywhere fancy really except the Navy Exchange and Commissary.

I won't knock him too much because he had the unwavering courage to leave the Philippines into a new country with no family or relatives. I truly admire that even to this present day. One of the stories my dad would share about joining the US Navy was, "My grandpa was a barber, my dad was a barber, I was a barber, and didn't want to be a barber forever, nor my kids to be barbers." So hence I respected that and never pursued that as a career.

Then one random day in sunny south San Diego when I was at my Uncle's house hanging out after playing with some of the neighborhood kids, he said, "Joe, there's this seminar coming up, you should check it out." Long story short, it was hosted by Robert Allen, author of Nothing Down For The 90s, and a few other books live event that was held in San Diego at the former KPBS recording studio. I am so glad I attended and listened to Robert and was automatically convinced that this was my answer to get rich!

As I mentioned I was still in high school at the time, but knew I had to figure this real estate game out. I didn't have any mentors, family, or friends in real estate, but I did some research and decided, let's go to Southwestern College in Chula Vista and take some real estate classes. Keep in mind that I was still in high school as a senior at Southwest High. I went to high school during the day and attended 3 different live classes at night weekly for a full semester.

Shortly, I was able to finish high school and my full semester at college with 3 courses: Real Estate Principles, Practice, and Appraisal. I kind of figured out that I should get these core classes so I can maybe help my credibility and perhaps get my real estate license. I wasn't quite sure. I just kept moving forward on my mission.

Simultaneously, I even started visiting open houses for REOs (real estate owned / bank foreclosed properties). Got on multiple realtor mailing lists. I was so close to purchasing one, but got scared. I saw what was going on in the news and the market was crashing. Similar to many of you, I bought too much into the fear. Little did I realize then, those are the times to be greedy as Warren Buffet would say, "Be fearful when others are greedy. Be greedy when others are fearful."

I gave in and let my fear take over and put real estate aside temporarily and continued onto San Diego State University for the next 4.5 years and was able to finish and get my Bachelors Degree. I had a few stories in between that did share some relevance, but I will save them for another book in the future on sales, cold calling, etc.

Let's fast forward a bit. When I decided to get a lot more serious about real estate again, I did have a job that to me was dead end and not very lucrative, maybe sounds quite familiar to some, right? So feeling very discontent at my day job, I decided to re-explore real estate. I chose to be a real estate agent because I had most of my classes to obtain my broker license, so I did.

When I started as a real estate agent in 1998, I was not very experienced, I didn't have too much knowledge about the industry, but what was going to be my saving grace in the industry was my pure HUNGER to succeed. Maybe it was my dad who kept saying, you got to be rich?!

Folks HUNGER will help you succeed in just about anything.

Deep down inside I still wanted to be an investor, but thought this was an easy way into the game. I could learn the ropes a bit. Then take it from there. Nervous about this whole commission ordeal as an agent, I started part-time while keeping my day job. I worked late nights and weekends until things started to click.

Remember, I always knew I wanted to be rich, but I wasn't quite sure how. I fired without necessarily aiming. At the time, I was very fortunate to have a great mentor who was very successful as a real estate agent. You know the stereotypical realtor driving a nice fancy car, dressing really nice, smelling good. He was selling 100s of homes yearly. I was obviously impressed by his success and toys because I didn't have any nice things like he did. However, when you pull back the kimono, I found out he was broke, having serious tax challenges, and a very terrible relationship with his girlfriend.

More importantly, he wasn't a great model for me as an investor. He didn't have any rentals! He did however, teach me to make money as an agent, lots of it as an agent. This I found very valuable where lots of skills you learn as an agent is very transferable to being an investor. Skills such as talking to people, closing techniques, lead generation, etc.

One day when I was at the office early dialing for dollars, also known basically as telemarketing on the phone, I got interrupted by a very disturbing phone call from his girlfriend interrogating me, "Where were you two last night?"

she asked. She went on speaking major nonsense, needless to say I left my realtor mentor / team leader immediately. I just couldn't take it anymore. We were at a listing appointment (someone wanted to sell their home) in case you were wondering. To me this was just unacceptable.

So a few years later with great training as an agent, I too became a very successful realtor myself, making six plus figures, and owning a home with equity, I decided to pull out $113,000 on a line of credit on my primary residence and decided to make a major run as I thought then I was going to become the long awaited investor.

From that money I was able to do several fix and flips, had several rentals (even several out of state), bought a multiplex myself, invested in a few syndications, was involved in a few apartment condo conversions, land developments, and even invested in several business start-ups. Sounds pretty cool, right? WRONG.

I was mainly a speculator. What is a speculator? Plain and simple, a dumb ass. I was getting really lucky on the appreciation of the market. I didn't know how to read proformas, look at TIMMUR, DSCR, IRR, Cash on Cash, etc.

As I said, what helped me previously was that *I was hungry*. I wanted to create a lifestyle for my family, which I did to some degree, having a 5000+ square foot home with a pool in a very exclusive neighborhood, some of my neighbors at the time were with the San Diego Chargers, we had multiple fancy cars, going on seriously cool vacations. However, the downfall was the residual / passive income was not necessarily there.

So folks, as you read this book please be absolutely clear to

BEGIN WITH THE END IN MIND.

How much do you truly need to sustain a great lifestyle? Where are you now financially? What are your household expenses? Mortgage payment? Car payment (s) ? Utilities? Groceries? Entertainment ? Plans for savings ? Retirement? College education ? Shopping sprees?

How about your business expenses? Staff ? Brick and Mortar ? Salaries ? Marketing? Coaching? Etc?

Let's just say for simplicity's sake = $7000 for household and $3000 to run your investment business. I would recommend at the bare minimum, use double that number to be your goal for passive / residual income.

This would equal:
$7000 + $3000 = $10,000 x 2 = $20,000 / monthly
= Enough passive income to be FINANCIALLY FREE.

Note: $10,000 is extra for just about anything. Additional reserves, emergencies, a great buffer so you never have to worry ever again!

Some folks start this journey without taking a good hard look at where they are at FIRST. Some folks even begin this journey thinking *I am going to be a billionaire.* Some folks think they need hundreds of thousands of doors.

I would argue most of you don't really need to own thousands of doors to become financially free. Be super crystal clear, how much do you really need? What kind of lifestyle do you want to attain? How soon do you want it? If you just keep going and going super driven without these ideas or foundations, truly, when will enough be enough? What are your current investments returning now? This could offset how many properties or cash flow that you really need.

Now realize that you don't have to be a certain age to accomplish this. I have made millions of dollars and truth be told I lost millions of dollars too because I wasn't at the time a good investor or money manager. What was even worse, had zero control of the market and didn't think the down cycle would last as long as it did.

I was purely an ambitious speculator. I didn't have the proper guidance, training, coaches, or mentors on being *fiscally fit* and financially responsible how to keep my money and assets and multiply it into even more. Fortunately, I slowly, but surely recovered, am a way smarter investor NOW than ever. I am clear on my direction in life and want to help YOU to get there.

Please take the time to figure this out. Get a coach or mentor to help you on this journey. Do some serious self-discovery, talk to your family, your significant other, what do they want too? Get their buy in and game over. If you're married, you know what they say, "Happy wife. Happy life!" You'll get there much quicker when they know what you're up to and willing to support you in any way. Even if it's simply to cheer you on.

My End Goal Is:

"Ninety Percent Of All Millionaires Become So Through Owning Real Estate. More Money Has Been Made In Real Estate Than In All Industrial Investments Combined. The Wise Young Man Or Wage Earner Of Today Invests His Money In Real Estate." - Andrew Carnegie

CHAPTER 2 - LIFESTYLE

A few years ago, I met this amazing person who eventually became one of my best friends in the world by the name of Hector Padilla. He and I met almost by accident. We were both at this real estate event for another amazing person - Tom Ferry. Both of us were coaches for Tom and both of us were top agents making significant incomes.

We were at one of Tom's events representing coaches and he asked us to hold these humongous placards with letters high in the sky. I forget why, but Hector coincidentally was right next to me and I just so happened to notice Hector with this weird expression on his face that was like, "WTF, this is ridiculous, why are we doing this?" I immediately said to him without hesitation, "Dude, just do it! Don't worry about it. It'll be over soon." Something to that regard. Maybe the conversation wasn't precise, but it's similar to how I remembered.

At any rate, Hector somehow respected me for saying that or thought, "who is this dude telling me what to do?" I am not sure, but we hit it off ever since.

Shortly after being a coach, Hector actually decided to move on to do other things - other really BIG things. We stayed in touch. He was also doing lots of flips at the time. He even had his own mini-boot camps. In these boot camps, he did what most of them do. Keep you in a room for a day or few days, take you on tours of projects, you know the drill.

It actually wasn't a turn off because I really respected him and considered him a friend. And even today Hector is still the real deal.

Fast forward, he got tired or got wiser, moved away from flips, and started investing in multifamily units, commercial, and a couple other bigger things. As I mentioned, him being a friend, we stayed in touch throughout the years and I started really paying closer attention to what he was doing.

Why? Most recently, Hector went out of the country 4 times in the year. That doesn't sound like a big deal? How about in addition they were all about 45 days on the average per trip to various countries! Meaning he took almost ⅓ of the year off! Now wouldn't you agree that is serious lifestyle to strive for?

Maybe that doesn't excite you, but figure out your ideal lifestyle.

Is it to go on mission trips and serve? Is it to help underprivileged youth or homeless people? As Tony Robbins said, "*live to give*".

Several years ago I sat on the Chula Vista Board of Directors. I felt this weird void in my life that I am making great money, but still there was this bit of emptiness in my life. Prior to joining, I met the director. One of the first few things he asked or mentioned was if you have "Time, talent, or treasure...you'll fit right in."

Do you have any of that - Time, Talent, Treasure? Or do you want more of either of those? Figure out your *future self.* Who will you be in the next 5 or 10 years? Tons can happen in such a short amount of time. Want to learn a new hobby, skill, or language? You can't do it because right now you don't have the time or money or both?

I'd invite you to do some soul searching or this simple exercise. Go to a quiet place. Maybe play some light classical music. Close your eyes and relax. Then start imagining yourself 5 or 10 years from now. What's your life look like? Who's around you? What are you driving? What are you wearing? How do you feel? Write this all down. Do this often. Do this daily for 5-30 minutes. However long you can focus is what I recommend.

I can go on and on with the questions you must know and answer. You MUST have the clarity. The more crystal clear the better. The last one I mentioned "feel" is extremely important. You can't just write things down or imagine it. You must actually live your future self in the moment of meditation or visualisation and have the feeling. The feeling is the juice. It's what will lubricate your brain and your muscles into action.

Having trouble visualizing? Some I know may be more motivated by pain than pleasure. So do the opposite. Imagine yourself broke, busted, and disgusted. Be so damn pissed off at yourself so you get inspired to do something.

Without knowing, there's no doing. Figure this out and MOVE.

JOE MENDOZA

My Dream Lifestyle Will Be:

"THE SIZE OF YOUR SUCCESS IS MEASURED BY THE STRENGTH OF YOUR DESIRE; THE SIZE OF YOUR DREAM; AND HOW YOU HANDLE DISAPPOINTMENT ALONG THE WAY." - ROBERT KIYOSAKI

CHAPTER 3 - K.I.S.S. - KEEP IT SIMPLE SILLY

They say in real estate if you want to find the deals, you must "*Kiss lots of frogs to find the deals or the prince*". I do truly believe that. Not everything you'll look at will be a deal. However, do keep this process simple.

Know your why, your goal, and then take action. Keep your processes simple. Keep this plan simple. The actions you do daily also should be simple. How many phone calls? How many letters? How many postcards? How many Letter of Intents? How many offers? How many bandit signs? How many door knocks?

These are important K.P.I.s - Key performance indicators to measure to keep you moving forward. There's a big difference between actively marketing and passively. I'd say active is more belly to belly. Talk to a real person. Don't just try to hide behind social media and doing videos. Even in so doing you'll need to eventually talk to a potential seller, agent, property manager, lead, or referral.

What will make it easier for you to accomplish this is DO NOT think you can do this by yourself. To some degree you can, but it won't be scalable and it won't create the lifestyle you want to create if you're just relying on you. What if you get sick? What if you want to go on vacation? Who's going to collect rents? Who's going to visit the properties? Who's going to make repairs on the properties? Who's going to evict bad tenants?

Two things that I will get into more later in the book:
1) People
2) Systems

Depending on your strategies or asset class you'll be going after in acquiring, I'd suggest starting to document your processes, creating checklists for yourself and others, and use these regularly for you and / or your team.

This way it's not just all in your head and you have to constantly reinvent your process or when you start getting really busy either you forget or your team.
Systems can be either you create as I mentioned via checklists or you buy them. Think of it this way. The word S.Y.S.T.E.M. can be broken down into an acronym:

Save
Your
Self
Time
Energy and
Money

How simple is that...silly? Simple to do. Simple not to do.

If you're relying 100% on memory, that I guarantee you is not scalable.

You take McDonald's for instance or Henry Ford and the Model T.

These both were systems driven. It's repetitive processes, organization, and efficiency.

This journey you are about to embark on or already on should be simple. Remember that a confused mind does nothing. If your goal is to make $10,000 monthly and let's just say each door on a single family home is making you $1000 net profit, how many doors do you need to hit your goal? Yes, 10.

If you have a day job, you typically work 8 hours a day. There's only 24 hours a day, right? How many hours can you devote to this? Yes, subtract, sleep, eat, family time. Then whatever time you have left, that's ok, use that time wisely, quit wasting it away on nonsense or things that won't help you hit your goals.

I hope this is making sense. It's simple with clarity. It's simple when you have a mentor. It's simple when you take the time to break things down to its smallest components.

I also would like to add, this is not a sprint or a get rich quick scheme. Remember the race between the Tortoise and the Hare? Who won?

Slow and steady does win provided that you stay focused and keep moving forward. I understand most people have jobs. There's good news and bad news about that. The good news is you can invest part-time and even more passively as I'll mention more later. If you want to be more proactive and hands on the bad news is that sometimes you won't have too much time to devote to this because you're stuck at your job and could get fired if you take too much time off or your work quality starts slipping.

Here's where you need people. Align yourself with people who can help Hire a VA a virtual assistant. Get help from family and friends. You have to have this unstoppable mindset that your WHY is way bigger than the how. If your why is strong enough, I guarantee you will find ways to figure out how to make this work. There are additional resources in the back of the book. I do suggest you check them out.

Think about it for just a second. I know people that prefer to generate their own deals, so they send out letters directly to owners. Not a bad idea by the way. Well, if you're at your day job, are you putting your cell phone on the letter or postcard?

I sure hope not! If you have a day job, a lead calls in from your letter, you can't answer because you might get fired, then what?

I have a few recommendations as I mentioned later in the book.

So keep your business of investing and acquisition simple...SILLY.

"REAL ESTATE CANNOT BE LOST OR STOLEN, NOR CAN IT BE CARRIED AWAY. PURCHASED WITH COMMON SENSE, PAID FOR IN FULL, AND MANAGED WITH REASONABLE CARE, IT IS ABOUT THE SAFEST

INVESTMENT IN THE WORLD."
- FRANKLIN D ROOSEVELT

CHAPTER 4 - JUST STARTING OUT

You are where you are for a reason. Don't make it wrong. It is what it is. However, something tells me that you want more since you're reading this book. First off, be grateful where you are. I'd be lying if I said the journey is easy, but remember if it were easy - more people would be doing it.

If you're currently renting, it's totally, ok. If you're broke and bad credit, it's ok too for now. It's NOT ok to stay that way forever.

Remember this nugget, there are 3 ingredients in investing in real estate:
1) Find The **Deal**
2) Have The **Dollars**
3) Have The **Knowledge**

If you have any one of those three, you're in! Let me explain.

You can search the internet, MLS, talk to agents, and lots of people and eventually land a deal, but don't have the money. You can talk to someone who has or makes lots of money, but didn't have the time to hunt for deals. That's where you come in and arrange some type of feasible partnership or get compensation for the deal. I'd recommend the partnership as this book is designed to help you accumulate wealth, passive income, and financial freedom…hopefully. Do this several times for a fee basis only eventually you don't necessarily have to need "money partners" any longer. This is a matter of personal preference, goals, and strategy. There's definite benefits AND negatives either your money or others.

Lastly, you can have the knowledge about the deal, the potential upside because of an insider secret of a lot or neighborhood, the knowledge that someone is about to sell, or the creativity to do the deal structure and that's where you can definitely come in. Any one of those three ingredients is critical to making investing happen.

Usually the knowledge taken to the next level may be creating a syndication or partnering or hiring a great real estate attorney. Talk about extreme knowledge and deal structuring. However, I have friends that aren't attorneys that are extremely creative and have made millions of dollars creatively deal structuring.

This is getting a little off topic, but that's the potential when you want to go really big fast.

So going more into basic, all of those ingredients you could "borrow" or "leverage" too…temporarily. How do I mean? I am about to have you think out of the box.

I know some folks that find existing AirBnBs that are NOT theirs and rent them out to others tens of hundreds of them! They take these deals and find short term tenants for them. They act almost as a property manager for the owner!

I know some folks that do *Lease Option / Rent To Own* that don't truly own the property and rent out the property to an end user and the money they make or arbitrage is called cash flow or profit to them! Now, both of those are pretty creative, right?

You served or are serving the military. Utilize your B.A.H. - Basic Allowance For Housing, purchase the property, and rent out the other rooms, also known as a "House Hack". Not in the military? How about FHA? I've spoken to many who had this hallucination or misconception that you have to have 20% down for purchasing a home. If you're a first-time buyer, you may qualify for 3.5% down or even ZERO down on specialized community or professional specific local or federally back government programs or grants.

Imagine purchasing a home for little to no down, renting out the rooms, while living in one, having the rent collected cover the mortgage, and even have some extra money in your pocket!

I have several friends that bought single family homes by nearby colleges that their kids attended. They had their child live in one room and rented out the other rooms. One particular friend of mine, upon graduating from college, he was given the home as a gift and he still has it today! I helped as a real estate agent here in San Diego. At the time the property nearby the University of California San Diego was originally purchased around $230,000. It is now worth over $800,000.

Do you have a child about to attend college? Am I giving you a great idea? I sure hope so!

Remember, be RESOURCEFUL. There's plenty of resources available in this world. Some folks get trapped in the scarcity mindset versus the abundance mindset. Find a way.

The most important thing is you start. Do you already have an existing home? Then pull out some equity on a cash out refinance or get a Line of Credit also known as an Equity Line. In 2004 I pulled out $113,000 in my existing primary residence.

I read the book **Rich Dad Poor Dad** by Robert Kiyosaki and was fired up on the concepts I learned in that one book. I then parlayed that money and in less than 2 years turned it into over $1 million dollars net worth with *ok* cash flow. That was a huge lesson in 2007-2009 when the market started turning.

Focus more on cash flow versus net worth. With net worth you can't take to the grocery store to buy food or pay bills. Cash flow is critically IMPORTANT. Can I say that again? CASH FLOW IS IMPORTANT. I'll get into numbers a little more later.

Remember the key is to get started, don't over analyze, don't be too scared. You can have any regular job and do any of the above I mentioned and even on a part-time out of state basis. How do I know? I've done it, I helped many of my family and friends do it. Many of them now are millionaires from what I shared and taught them.

They still have regular jobs and building even more wealth, buying more property, saving, and investing in other ways too. In other words , you don't have to all of sudden be this real estate guru, philanthropist, selling programs on youtube, or late night infomercials. I'm teasing. If that's what you want to do, so be it. This might sound a little like me?!

Just invest in a plex or more and create that lifestyle you are seeking.

"BE FEARFUL WHEN OTHERS ARE GREEDY, AND GREEDY WHEN OTHERS ARE FEARFUL." - WARREN BUFFET

CHAPTER 5 - DEEPER DIVES INTO THE PLEXES - ONE TO FOUR VERSUS 5+

DuPLEX, TriPLEX, FourPLEX. In real estate, these are 2,3, and 4 units respectively usually under one roof. Very similar to a "House Hack" as mentioned earlier, but in the true sense they are actual separated units.

These are really great for starting out. Same concepts as the House Hack, but stepping it up a notch.

It is categorized as One To Four especially for lending purposes. Lenders consider these under a Residential versus Commercial. Here are some of the differences. When you go into 5+ units lenders in some cases think that it's less risky. Why? Think of it this way.

When you have 4 doors or a 4plex, one unit is vacant, you are losing 25% of the income or cash flow versus 75% that you are retaining. You go lower into 3, 2 or even 1, your risk and the "losses" are exponentially higher. When you have one rental, a single door, and it's vacant, you are responsible for 100% of the mortgage payment to the lender.

Unfortunately or fortunately, I had a hard lesson in the 2007-2009 mortgage meltdown. I had several properties during that era throughout the United States, specifically Texas, Florida, Nevada, and California. I had plenty of reserves in the beginning. However, one person stopped paying me rent, then another, and then another. My savings / reserves were rapidly depleting.

When you have 100 doors and 5 are vacant, that's only 5% vacancy and often times when you invest right, even if those doors or units are empty for long periods of time you can still cash flow because the other units that are occupied are enough to cover the debt service or mortgage payment to the bank. Are you starting to realize that sometimes more doors makes more sense? You just have to know your goals.

I know some investors who at 5 to 10 doors are financially free. They chose not to partner with anyone or participate in a syndication (we'll talk more on this later). They got super hyper focused. They bought slow and steady one home per year. Then aggressively paid them all off re-investing the extra cash flow they were getting. Most often, never refinanced the properties, pulled cash out, or took lines of credits on any of the properties they bought.

Just remember the race between The Tortoise and The Hare – slow and steady the tortoise won that race! Buy one rental at a time, know your numbers, and pay those properties off quickly!

How long could you sustain? As I write this today, we are in 2020, probably one of the worst global uncertainties of my lifetime. We are dealing with this "invisible enemy" called

CoronaVirus or Covid19. There are government rules in place such as *No Eviction Moratoriums* essentially, allowing tenants not to pay for certain periods of time. However, guess who has to pay or suffer serious consequences of potential foreclosure for not paying the lender? You guessed it, YOU!

So definitely, think about reserves. Watch your numbers carefully monthly.

We will get a little more into these numbers later. Lenders require on qualifying that you do have "reserves". I require that you have reserves! I am being transparent as real estate investing is risky, but you can mitigate your risks, by implementing some of these ideas and true stories I am sharing.

When you go for more doors, 5+ on up, the economies of scale work in your favor, and usually even easier to manage. For instance, at 16+ doors, an on-site, living in one of the units property manager can be available to help you manage your property and also be somewhat of a guard dog helping you protect and maintain your investment.

I was coaching a gentleman awhile back who had 90 doors free and clear. The good news was the properties were all free and clear. The bad news he was self-managing, they were ALL single family detached homes, and spread out all over the city.

I kept telling him to do a 1031 on them into one or less roofs. Basically trade up to an Apartment Complex, hire a property manager, be the asset manager, and ENJOY LIFE. He and his wife were always getting into arguments, about repairs, visiting properties from one side of the city, to the complete opposite side of the city, wasting away valuable resources, and time.

Remember Chapter 3? If not, do please go back and re-read. K.I.S.S. You must keep this game or plan simple. Otherwise, you may lose your mind, get divorced, or have to give up your investments that you worked so hard to obtain.

I've had multiple clients and several purchases because people did not know what they were getting into, got in over their head, did not take the time to *learn before they earned*, too cheap to hire real professionals : Agents, Property Managers, Attorneys, Advisors, etc. Their "do it yourself" mentality works to some degree, but truly, how much is your time worth? This is THE MOST VALUABLE ASSET you must protect at all times at all costs.

One roof, multiple doors. There are many, many, other books that go into this. This book is mainly to stimulate your taste buds and maybe get you to TAKE ACTION.

CHAPTER 6 - OTHER ASSET CLASSES

There are many different asset classes you can pursue to make a run for this goal. Most people buy a rental, then a small plex, then multifamily apartments. This is the normal progress. Some jump right into multiple units right out of the gates. Almost all the time they do this via what they call a syndication - simply pooling other peoples moneys and leveraging other people's credit to buy these multimillion dollar assets.

There's also mobile home parks. This is simply renting out a plot of dirt or the space. This is very attractive as you won't have the typical expenses associated with single family homes or multi units. Your expenses may simply be utilities and water.

The resident will typically own their single or double wide house on wheels as some would say. You won't have to worry about maintenance and upkeep as that is their own personal property. Now the value add potential here would be usage of laundry facilities, maybe storage space, you can even perhaps set up a dog park area for their pets. Sometimes you can improve the landscaping, the signage, the driveways and if there's only dirt roads place asphalt or improve the roads by doing reslurry.

Storage units can also be another asset class to consider. You're simply renting out an enclosed space, sometimes dirt, or even a parking spot. A While back I had a 18.5 Sea Swirl fishing boat. I loved that toy! Unfortunately, I lived in a neighborhood where there were CC&Rs - Covenants Conditions, and Restrictions, basically rules of the neighborhood. Essentially, you cannot park and leave a boat in your driveway for long periods of time. So guess where my boat was?

Yes, at the storage facility! I was paying just a little over $200 a month to keep it there. Believe it or not, some people keep storage units for years at a time. Unfortunately, I was one of them. During the mortgage meltdown in 2007-2009, I moved out of this massive home of over 5,000 square feet into this two bedroom apartment. It was a very humbling experience as I may add.

Long story short, I thought that this setback was going to be minor and short. Unfortunately, being at the epicenter of the collapse (as a realtor at the time), it was a really long road to recovery not just for me, but for America . Some of you may have remembered that. Some I know never recovered.

I do want to point out this massive lesson of the time. The ones that got hit really hard for instance were those heavily invested in stock NOT real estate. There were many folks that were in their last stage of life who lost half their portfolio or in some cases 80-90% of their liquidity. This is important to point out as yes, you could sell, short sale, or even walk away from a property or properties and in a few short years recover, like some folks actually did.

However, if you're in your latter part of life, you may not have the physical energy to go back to work, stockpile the cash, and recover. This was the tragedy that was realized by most of the seniors during that era.

Here's the good news. If you invest right, really be conservative with your numbers, these assets will take care of you for the rest of your life. Imagine having a home fully paid off. What's the cash flow? Anywhere from $1000 to maybe $5000 or more a month? It won't matter if there's a meltdown in the economy. People will still need a place to live, right?

I really want you to think about that and how crucial it is to invest in real estate.

Another niche versus an asset class is renting out these properties more like a business. Here are some suggestions: AirBnB, Student Housing, Assisted Living, Work-Force Housing (travelling nurses and other professions). Think about it. Some of these pay a major premium for the rooms you can rent out or units. In some cases government agencies or large corporations will pay even "per bed". How much? $1000 or more per bed!

Are you going to control your destiny or leave it up to a financial person who sometimes has way less assets than you do? What are their fees? What are they invested in? I was in the same building with one of those financial guys. We had those water cooler talks every now and then. One day he shared most of his assets were in real estate. Go figure! He had more than a dozen homes all fully paid off!

Please folks heed my advice. I am not totally opposed to the stock market. Just diversify.

The Asset Class I Am Most Interested In Or Will Focus On Is:

CHAPTER 7 - BUILD A TEAM

I've always said, "Teamwork makes the DREAM work." How true is this statement in this endeavor? 100% the truth. You cannot do this business alone. Real estate investing is a team sport. If you are in another trade or different business, you'll definitely need a mentor, coach, or someone to guide you to help you speed up the process or mitigate risk.

You don't think you need one? So go ahead and try it. You may or not make it, but I will say this. "Your EGO, should not be your amigo." Usually I've noticed, when someone doesn't want coaching or a mentor, it's almost always tied to this statement. What normally follows next is this, "I can figure it out" or "I know". Folks, that is your EGO talking.

Be humble enough to respect those that already made the mistakes, those that learned better easier ways, will help you on this journey and accelerate the process, and also mitigate your risk. Please be careful who you work with if you do decide to hire a mentor or coach because who you work with does matter.

Have they accomplished what you'd like to accomplish? Can they hold you accountable? Do they have things you want to have? Are they living the way you want to live? Have they travelled places you want to go? Is their net worth, liquidity, passive income, where you want to be? If so, then hire them! If not, fire them! I mean this sincerely.

Once upon a time I was that guy at one point too. I was like that fly trying to escape through the window that kept hitting my head on the window not realizing there was an opening to the left and right. This is a pure example of insanity. You keep doing the same things over and over hoping and praying for a different result. You definitely need a coach or mentor. If not me, find someone!

How about even a realtor or broker? They can help you deal source. They have access to Multiple Listing Service (MLS) and even potentially Costar (this is more for commercial real estate). Don't disrespect them either. What do I mean? In 2008-2012 when there were tons of REOs and Short Sales, I was working with dozens of investors and cash buyers. The ones that respected me, saw the deals first. The ones that asked for discounts on my commission or kickbacks was maybe a one and done.

Some of them truly shocked me. I found them a great deal via my methods of letters, cold calling, door knocking, advertising, etc. I spent my hard earned money that they didn't have to. Sure I would make a 3% or 6% commission which in some cases was $10,000 to $20,000. Then they had the ability to make $100,0000 to $200,000 on their flip (which some actually did with me). Then the disrespectful ones had the audacity to ask me for a break or concession? How dare they? That was pretty insulting.

You are killing the golden goose laying the golden eggs for you when you do something like this. Don't be penny pinching. You're picking up pennies and tripping over dollars tens of hundreds of thousands of dollars! Be kind to realtors, brokers, and wholesalers out there. Don't be so short-sighted, play the long game. This is not a sprint, it's a marathon.

Do you have a 9 to 5 job? Are you married and have kids? Well, you may only have 10 to 20 extra hours per week or sometimes even less than that to work on investing. It won't take too many hours to do this provided you have great people on your team.

I'd even suggest having an assistant whether in-house or a virtual assistant to help you. They can do research, set up your marketing campaigns, just about everything you can imagine. How much is your time worth? That is what you should consider to help get more things done in a day versus you trying to do it all.

Time is your most precious valuable asset. Your minutes on this planet are non-refundable. When they are gone, you can never get them back.

You have the ability to make thousands of dollars or more a month from investing. In order to get there you must invest in yourself and other people. How about managing the property? Property managers should be on your team too. They usually charge 3% on up per month. On residential property the norm is 6 to 8% of the monthly rents collected. Are you going to do this yourself? Guess what, it's not as easy as you would think. Here are some other considerations: Do you know the current laws especially when it comes to screening tenants? Do you know how to evict someone properly if they stop paying rent?

By doing this part yourself, you will slowly lose the ability to acquire more cash flowing assets and take a much longer time to hit your goal. Having a realtor and property manager are essential to this business. How about an attorney? Do not get agreements or contracts online. Especially when it comes to partnership, borrowing other people's money, or raising private capital for bigger acquisitions. There are no typical boilerplate agreements. Nothing is usually typical when it comes to the bigger units and plexes. If there is no broker and you're buying directly from a seller or owner, I highly advise you to get an attorney involved to put the paperwork together, review it, or both.

Be sure that they specialize in real estate, contract, syndication, or securities law. This does depend on your strategy at the time. When it comes to larger acquisitions, 100s of doors, mobile home parks, shopping centers, storage units, industrial, you know those larger types of assets, those acquisitions are a lot more complicated then a single family single property acquisition. The agreements especially if you utilize creative financing, seller carry, lease option are definitely more intensive which you really should bring a great reputable attorney on your team. Just like realtors, not all attorneys are created the same. Who you work with does matter. Ask for a referral and do some research before you hire.

Another thing especially with realtors on the basic level, remember this truth. They are NOT all created the same. Just because they know how to close a sale doesn't mean they understand investment real estate. Doesn't mean when they offer you a discount or kickback that you should use them. Ask them if they even own a home. Ask them if they have a rental or rentals. How many? How long have they been investing? Where have they invested? Who have they helped? Do they know what cap rate means? Do they understand a proforma? Timmur?

If they have this weird look on their face and try to skirt their way out of the answer, run! Seriously, just because you like them, doesn't mean they're any good! A friend of mine once shared a story with me about her poor friend. Her poor friend was seriously taken advantage of. A realtor convinced her to sell her property in California. She bought one locally and used the rest of the cash proceeds to buy a multifamily out of state where the agent recommended and got a referral fee. He convinced her that this was absolutely a great deal without even thoroughly analyzing the numbers.

Not even a year later, she was hemorrhaging cash. The property wasn't cash flowing even when it was fully occupied. Every single month this poor woman had to come out of pocket to make sure she didn't get foreclosed by the bank. What was even worse, she was in her retirement years. She was expecting this to be her nest egg, cash flow passively to supplement her income. This was the exact opposite. Her true nest egg was getting depleted to fund this losing investment.

That realtor ONLY thought about himself and the commission. A good realtor will give all options and back them up why or why not to proceed. Sure everyone can have their opinion, but I want you to also take responsibility, TRUST, BUT VERIFY. I will go more into this on the Due Diligence section.

As you can see, building a team is imperative, also having

the right, credible, reliable people on the team is just as important. Again, don't have them on the team just because they sound like you, dress, like you, could laugh at your jokes, they must be able to be brutally honest with you, not just tell you things you want to hear. This might be a shameless plug, but a great coach can do that. When you hire a great coach, most will be very direct with you. They might even hurt your feelings, but they'll save you thousands and sometimes millions of dollars in this business. If you do hire a coach, remember, you didn't hire them because you needed more friends.

Do you know DISC? This is extremely important in building your team. Tony Robbins is a pretty reliable source for this test. Simply type in "DISC Tony Robbins". On his website, anyone could pretty much take his test online. Do spend the extra money for the more intensive results.

There are other tests out there: Predictive Index, Behavioral Tests, Cognitive Assessments, etc. My message here is that you must know who you are, what your strong suits are, what you like, or dislike, what should you delegate, or who should you hire to pick up where you are deficient or tasks you shouldn't be doing.

I know for me, I am typically a strong D.I. Very strong driver and Influencer. Depending on what I am working on or where I am in my career, these are usually things I should be doing when in my natural ability - leading, managing, selling. Usually with the S and C, they are the numbers and analytical folks, like administrative staff, accountants, the engineer type...typically. Just realize everyone is a little bit of everything. Some folks are clearly strongly suited to one category over another. It usually depends on where they are in life and their career.

Do keep in mind that this is not the end all solution as sometimes if someone really knows and understands this test, they can actually manipulate the answers to gear more towards the position they are applying for. So do be careful and aware with that said.

Knowing who you are and who you should bring on the team will help keep your sanity and become more successful at this or actually any business. There are times where I can put on the SC hat, but it usually takes longer than someone with this strong suit. I can get it done and do realize I am not the best at it. So I will employ that help as needed.

For example, when working high level analytics, building up spreadsheets, working on accounting, building up proformas, or running numbers, I have people on my team that will do that for me way faster and correctly versus me who might take two to three times longer to do the same job. The one thing I am clear on is I have to make sure I really understand what all the data means. I will trust, verify, and create the strategy to make sure it works in favor of my investors, partners, or myself then decide if it's a deal and if we should move forward on the acquisition.

Bottom line (this is what usually Drivers say by the way) build a team. You don't need another job. Focus on your HBUT - Highest Best Use of YOUR time. There are only 24 hours in a day folks. This is a business you can build to help get you more time and freedom. Build it like one.

Add These Names To Your Contact List:

My realtor / broker is:

My attorney is:

My lender is:

My insurance name is:

My contractor is:

My handyman is:

My termite company:

My painter:

My flooring / carpet company is:

My plumber is:

My electrician is:

My carpenter is:

CHAPTER 8 - DEAL HUNTING

There's lots of ways to find your potential investments. I will start by saying realtors and brokers are good, but do remember they don't have equal skills and abilities. The barrier of entry in most cases is too easy to become one. In California for instance, you take a few classes, take a crash course, apply to the state (provided you don't have a serious criminal record), pass the test, and in a period of about 3 months, you could sell single family homes or multi-million dollar commercial properties! Pretty simple, right? It actually is to get a license. However, to become a real pro in the industry, it takes quite a bit more.

To the highest degree there's multiple designations, additional training, some serious realtors even hire coaches like myself. I was coached by some of the most successful agents, brokers, business owners, and leaders of the nation. Then eventually I too became a coach.

One day I was sitting in the San Diego Country Club in Chula Vista California. I was taking a break from coaching and happened to be at an event with Tom Ferry as the speaker. At the time, I was selling roughly 50 homes and making about $500,000 a year. I was moved by Tom and asked him to be my personal coach. He asked me several questions to screen me out. Then he said, "why do you want me?" I said, "I want to sell 100 homes and make $1,000,000 this year." He saw I was deadly serious and agreed. "Ok, Joe $3000 a month, we start next week."

Within about 3 months he says to me, "Joe, you're going to hit it no matter what. Do you want to be one of my coaches?" The rest was history. I've been a coach for over ten years now. I fell in love with giving back and seeing people succeed. That year by the way in case you're wondering, 2005 I sold 113 homes, made $1.1m NET, was number 7 in Southern California for Prudential California Realty, and Top 1% in the nation.

In other words again, no realtors are or should be treated equally.

If you work with someone like me, very seasoned, has a pulse on the market, has a team, and through connections and thousands of dollars spent on tons of marketing will have access to many deals! I would add treat them with respect. I guarantee you, you won't be the only investor they will be working with so maybe enough create some incentives for them why they should work with you. Don't think it's the other way around, just because you have money you're special.

Trust me, I know lots of people with money. It's way harder to find deals.

If you want to do the lead generation yourself I suggest letters, cold calling, and door knocking as my top ideas. Get ready to put some sweat equity, face tons of rejection, and get down and dirty. You think it's easy doing what realtors do, NO WAY I've been at this game through the ups and downs for almost 30 years now. This is what we do to get the listings or deals.

Can you be successful at investing? Of course you can! When your WHY is strong enough, you'll find the HOW. On mailers, there's companies out there that can do them for you. You can even use your printer and do them yourself. I strongly recommend doing hand written envelopes in blue ink. There's more mystique to force someone to open it when the letter looks more personalized.

Now having the right mail list is very important too. Don't just spray and pray these letters into random neighborhoods. I have several resources in the back of the book. You must go after some of the low hanging fruit, like probates, divorces, high equity owners, expired listings, for sale by owners, etc.

Cold calling is another method to deal source. Respectively, KNOW YOUR STATE AND LOCAL laws. If someone is on the DNC list, DO NOT CALL. There are heavy fines tied into these violations. Some that choose to ignore what I say and take their chances, this is up to you to endure the consequences. You should be fairly well scripted if you are going to do this. Don't just ramble on and on. Remember also WIIFM. People are always listening to one radio station, "What's In It For Me?" I have more resources on this as well in the back of the book.

On door knocking, this is where you may have some serious degrees of separation from anyone. First off, it's exercise. That's a great way to look at it. Secondly, you really have to be on it when you are face to face. Thirdly, talk about thick skin. You will get rejected lots of times, be ready for it. Realize a NO, means on to the next. Never ever take anything personal. They will say the meanest things sometimes, be ready for it, and brush it off. Here's a bonus, make them laugh. Yes, I mean that.

Think about it. When you or you try to get someone or your kids to laugh, doesn't it change the mood? Practice, practice, practice this! Participate in Stand Up comedy, Improv, or Toastmasters. This truly helps! How do I know? Yes, I can put checkboxes on those!

Referrals. Tell everyone what you're up to. Don't be a silent investor. You know what they say, "Fake it until you make it." You don't have to lie, just let them know you are in the process of investing or moving some of your current assets into more solid investments or something of that sort. You'd be surprised. Some folks actually don't like realtors. As I mentioned before, the barrier of entry is TOO EASY. Oftentimes, when some weren't as committed to their profession as I, didn't work on skills to become a professional, or were lucky enough to find some great mentors, coaches, or leaders, were improperly trained, this I am sure left a bad impression on these folks.

That means good news for you if you act professionally and treat people with respect. You can deal source yourself!

Treat others the way you want to be treated. I can assure you massive success in any business following this simple rule.

"LAND MONOPOLY IS NOT ONLY MONOPOLY, BUT IT IS BY FAR THE GREATEST OF MONOPOLIES; IT IS A PERPETUAL MONOPOLY, AND IT IS THE MOTHER OF ALL OTHER FORMS OF MONOPOLY." - WINSTON CHURCHILL

CHAPTER 9 - G.I.G.O. GARBAGE IN GARBAGE OUT

During 1990 to 1995 I was attending San Diego State University. It was an amazing era to be a student. Hall of Famer NFL player Marshall Faulk was in attendance. Our football games were insane watching him play. We were voted #2 party school in the nation. Playboy magazine was even on campus as well doing photoshoots! As a young adult, these were some fun times for sure!

I learned so much at SDSU on top of those other memorable experiences. Folks that say or don't believe in college or higher education. Here is my belief. Sure it's not for all. However, this is why people should attend. You will learn how to start and finish a great goal. Whether it is 4 years or more, just finishing and getting your degree is a major accomplishment. It doesn't even matter the degree. You will form disciplines, learn how to deal with different personalities, learn more about other cultures, ideas, have tenacity, laser focus, learn responsibility, have and earn respect from many.

I did finish and it definitely wasn't easy. My parents only gave me $500 total the whole time I was there. The rest was funded with loans, grants, having as many as 3 jobs one semester, and I even had to borrow one time from my amazing Auntie Margie Brown (big shout out for your mom and you Joey B)!

Yes, one time I was between a rock and a hard place. My mom said she didn't have any money and I was past due on my tuition. "Go ask your Auntie Margie if she can help," she said. I was lucky, she sure did help me and am forever grateful. Without her, I probably would have not made it that semester.

At any rate, one of my classes in college I learned this extremely valuable lesson G.I.G.O. Garbage In Garbage Out. I am going to date myself right now. I was taking this Computer Information Systems 101 class learning Lotus 123. Yes, some can remember this one archaic program. It's basically really BASIC excel before there was the intuitive and advanced Microsoft Excel spreadsheets that we have today.

My professor was a fellow named Mr Foster who led our class. He was quite a heavy set, short tempered, man who ran his class old school. I remember one time one of my classmates wasn't paying attention and busy disrupting the class. Mr Foster took his chalk and threw it at the student! How's that technique for making people pay attention?

Despite his methodology of teaching I did learn that if you put one wrong number in the cell, or reverse minus symbol versus plus, or screw up the formula, your entire sheet would be wrong.
How is this relevant? In real estate investing, you must know and even fall in love with numbers. It can truly make

you or break you. Attention to detail is an absolute must!

If you run a regular spreadsheet and make one mistake, you originally think it's a deal when in actuality it's a dud, you've screwed up, and maybe will be the greater fool on this so-called deal! Know or create some Rules Of Thumb or Key Performance Indicators (KPIs).

There's actual software and subscriptions out there to make this whole process easier. Remember time could be major money in this business. There are resources in the back of this book, be sure to check them out.

You can spend hours or days creating spreadsheets and formulas or you could spend 5 to 10 minutes per deal. Depending on the demands of the market, sometimes it's a 200 to 1 ratio. Meaning you'll have to look at 200 deals and spreadsheets to finally acquire that one deal. Do the math. Would you rather spend one day looking at 10 to 20 deals or 1 month and only be able to analyze 1 to 2 deals because you were old fashioned or too cheap to get the software or right tools for your business? How bad and how fast do you want it?

Just look at it as a cost of doing business. Great people + great systems = Success and Scalability.

"LANDLORDS GROW RICH IN THEIR SLEEP." - JOHN STUART MILL

CHAPTER 10 BE A PAIN IN THE ASK

I am a firm believer that persistence breaks down resistance. My kids who I love very much and probably your kids for this matter are perfect examples of this. They were about 5 and 3 at the time and wanted a dog so bad. Every single day I would hear, "Dad, I want a dog." My daughter even went out of her way to write a contract, "I will pick up the poop. I will feed it. I will walk it." etc etc. Now how can you say no to that? Yes, I eventually surrendered.

Here's the bonus for my investor mindset, *I love deals and so should you.* I went on to Craigslist. Then went into the For Sale section and typed in "Free Dog". Yes, I did! Crazy how sometimes the law of attraction works. I happened to see a pure bred Shih Tzu who needed a home! The owner lived in a small apartment. They were always so busy and shared with me he was living in a crate most of the time. They felt so bad that they were willing to give him up. We ended up with a sweetheart who's been with us over 10 years!

How does this relate? You must be relentless in this business especially if you know it's a great deal or purchase.

As a broker, I once had a client who wanted to sell his 17 unit office building in Escondido California. He was at his retirement age and tired of self-managing. He wanted to cash out, move to Hawaii, and retire. He wanted a premium price a little above market. I warned him it would be a challenge, but if he entertained some creativity we'd have a better chance.

Several offers came in the first few weeks and months I had the listing. He shut them all down. However, there was one buyer who made an offer with a seller carryback option. He knew the property was free and clear, so he offered he'd bring $400,000 to the table and requested the seller be the bank or carry the rest of the note.

Again my seller shut it down. He didn't fully understand the terms and conditions on a carry. He was so adamant about his price. I did get him his price, but he didn't like the terms. A few more months go by. No other offers came close to this investor's offer with the carry.

I insisted he take it. He finally did. The buyer was a *pain in the ask* and so was I. Remember a no now doesn't mean a "no" later. Sometimes you must keep following up, making the calls, sending the letters to agents, sellers, and landlords to get the real deals.

By doing so, you will reap the rewards. Remember, do today what others won't to live tomorrow how others can't. You must be comfortable being uncomfortable. This is where the true magic happens in this business.

CHAPTER 11 - VALUE ADD

What is value add? Think in terms of ARV. For single family homes and condos, it's the After Repaired Value. For commercial, apartments, and multifamily, I like to refer to it as the After Repositioned Value. What's nice about commercial real estate is you could what investors would refer to as *forced appreciation.* When you do any kind of value add that leads to increased cash flow, you forced the value up, purposely in a good way! You didn't have to wait for interest rates to go down, something great to happen to the neighborhood or community, you simply added value to the property, which attracted higher paying residents, which increased cash flow, which forcibly increased the value of the property!

Have you ever watched HGTV and see those fix and flip reality shows? There definitely is some truth to it. Like being under budget, the drama, and disconnect with your team. No one said this business is easy. You will have to know what you are getting into before making it official and purchasing.

What are the rehab costs involved? Could you do some light and easy cosmetic repairs or changes? Is carpet and paint enough? Remember curb appeal. When anyone does a quick drive by, are the weeds too tall they can't even see your For Rent sign or number to call? How's the driveway? Do we need to repave? Do we need to cut some trees down to open it up a bit, maybe even see a view in some rooms?

How about the interior? How's the floor? How about the subfloor? How about the foundation? Now this is an interesting one. Thankfully it didn't cost me too much. Several years ago, I represented a seller. He told me he replaced the carpet throughout the house. Trusting him I put "newer carpet" on the description. Long story short the sale went through, I got paid my commission, a few months later I got a disturbing message.

The new owner filed a lawsuit against me and my brokerage. Now that didn't go after the seller who they should've, they went after the "deeper pockets". The seller essentially lied on the Transfer Disclosure Statement. They did change the carpet however, they should've noticed and stated there were cracks in the foundation!

The new owner discovered the cracked slab when they decided to change the carpet. Of course they were upset! The seller filled out the Transfer Disclosure Statement also known as a TDS and one of the questions was "Are you aware of any defects on the house…cracked foundation." This is not verbatim, every state has different forms, rules, and disclosures, but something to definitely look out for on any purchase.

Needless to say, the judge during the lawsuit chose the plaintiff over us.

Some of the lessons here, an agent or broker is a good buffer to some degree on either side whether you're a buyer or seller. We could've got nasty and sued our seller, but that wouldn't be kosher and would not be good publicity. We simply licked our wounds and kept trucking.

When you do value adds or rehab. Do things right, not necessarily expensive. Get quality people who do quality work. Pay attention during the process. Ask lots of questions with your contractors, handyman, sellers, and if you do have the opportunity the current and existing tenants.

Will the addition or modification increase my cash flow? By how much? By when? How soon can I recoup that cost? Don't go overboard either. Look at neighbors in the existing area. Look at competition rentals in the area. It does make a difference who your end user is and what are their likes and dislikes. Remember this a rental, not the house you'll be living in and sleeping in everyday.

Someone once said, "Live where you want to live. Invest where it makes money." There is definitely lots of truth to that. However, don't be that "slumlord". Treat people right. Call them "residents" versus "tenants". You respect them, they'll respect you, and your investment!

Stick to neutral colors and don't be too trendy. If you know it's a high foot traffic area, stay away from carpet. In some cases, go with the tile versus linoleum. Again think of the long game. Speaking of long game, consider 3 year leases or more minimum.

If you have a rental that there's constant turnover, like potentially student housing, think about all the things you have to repair or replace to "make ready" for the next resident. I remember when my brother rented a single family detached home. He rented out one room and several other of his fraternity brothers rented out the other rooms. I walked in there on a random visit and thought oh my! There were definite signs of some crazy good parties going on in there! Yikes is correct! I'm not opposed to college or student housing.

I actually do have a rental that I personally managed. It is a room of four and four very responsible students live in. Now the catch is I got every single one of their parents on the lease, did the proper screening, etc. It helps when you have the resources and are in the profession. They've never caused any problems, always are extremely good on communication, and want to stay for several years until they finish college, and next have their siblings take over! Talk about win / win / win!

Some of your past beliefs, maybe about student housing as a potential plex of yours hopefully got demolished with my GREAT experience. Also, it was quickly rented because of the close proximity to the university! Here was the bonus, these young men shared that they kept getting turned down and turned away by many other property managers and landlords because of multiple reasons: no rental history, high risk, some places didn't allow cosigners, or multiple tenants unrelated, as they were so grateful when I agreed to them. Their parents were extremely supportive and grateful as well!

"DON'T WAIT TO BUY REAL ESTATE, BUY REAL ESTATE AND WAIT." - WILL ROGERS, ACTOR

CHAPTER 12 - DUE DILIGENCE

This is one of the most important steps in this whole process. This may be your last opportunity to hit the eject button without penalty. In California and on single family homes, there's a 17 day *free look* grace period even automatically written in our California Association of Realtors Residential Purchase Agreements. During this time, you could pretty much back out for any reason.

I had one client one time back out because she found cockroaches during the inspection. I am sure there was more to that as I later found out, but yes you have the ability to back out as long as you are still within the allotted time frames. Sometimes sellers or listing agents may shorten that time frame, so do look very closely on the counters going back and forth.

I highly recommend hiring a licensed, seasoned, properly trained Home Inspector with great reviews to inspect any properties you are purchasing even if a home were newer like less than a year old. Go figure. If they haven't owned the property one year, why are they selling so quickly? Is there something potentially wrong with the property? A great agent would normally suggest at least 3 different inspectors or you can go about and choose your own via Yelp, Google, or referral.

The reason why you don't want them just recommending one is you don't want the agent influencing the inspector on your purchase or appear to be influencing the inspector. For example, any material facts or defects a real estate agent could potentially coerce or bribe the inspector not to point it out.. This may or may not happen, but if they personally only recommended one, in the court and judges eyes, they would typically construe this as potentially manipulation of a transaction. This is not good if it is a surprise! There's a serious defect with the home or commercial property!

However, "caveat emptor" buyer beware. You still should have your guards up to make sure you are carefully looking throughout the entire property , reading all the disclosures, and reading all inspections, homeowner association documents, termite, and appraisal.

Yes, there is a lot! This is your investment. Take care of it, it will take care of you.

On commercial property it's even more intense. There's a Phase 1 and Phase 2 reports. These are more expensive than a home inspection report. They go into the Environment Impacts of the property, the land, and the surroundings. Is there potentially an endangered species nearby or on the land? Well, I guess you can't do an expansion on the property now. Was the property a former gas station or built on a landfill? What are the current conditions of the property? Does it have costly or potentially expensive repairs, maintenance, etc Now with those considerations, should we now bring a Soils Specialist, an architect, or civil engineer? How do we build that into our spreadsheet analysis? Will we still get a good return making these repairs, modifications, or additions?

This is exactly why I mentioned earlier on Team Building. How can you possibly know all this or learn it and be an expert in these other areas of this business? Do you think it's expensive hiring a professional? The biggest tragedy is to bypass any one of these during the Due Diligence phase or go cheap and have a property defect bite you in the rear later.

CHAPTER 13 - FINANCING

This will be a tip that you MUST remember. Then decide on your strategy and stick to it. When you are looking for deals or acquisitions, you pretty much should go after the no-brainers. Here's what I mean. You are either going to do the following from here on out. You stick to this Rule of Thumb, you'll do ok:

1) Buy it because it's a great **PRICE**.
2) Buy it because you have incredible **TERMS**.

Yes, that's pretty much it. If you pay all cash, I sure hope you're getting under market price. Know the comparables or comps in the area. Do not just rely on Zillow. I know certain states that may be a non-disclosure state. However, there are resources out there how you can potentially find the answers you are looking for. Be sure to look them up in the back of the book.

Why should you make sure it's a great price? Money, just like in today's market is super cheap! Depending on when you are reading right now it's under 3% . If you pursue a property anywhere above that number they have a higher existing cap rate, you can borrow the money and make the spread or also known as arbitrage.

For instance, you are looking at a multiple family property. Market cap and the actual cap of the property is 10% or more. The Cap Rate is essentially the net operating income divided by the purchase price.

Remember **"IRV":** (Net Operating) Income / (Cap) Rate = Value (Purchase Price)

Still don't understand this? Go to Youtube or GTS (Google This Stuff) Knowing the IRV formula can help also in your Due Diligence phase. How will you know if you are getting a deal? This really pertains to multiplexes. When you go larger or move away from single family homes and condos, the investment strategy is "does it pencil out".

When a property is paid in cash, the cap rate is more like the percentage on the return of that cash based on the Gross Rents minus ALL expenses divided by the price of the property. Is this clear as mud? I will re-emphasize if it isn't this is exactly why you need a team.

If you can't pay all cash, yes, you must talk to a bank and get a loan. The good news is that if you buy 5 or more units, the bank will really pay attention to the performance of the property. They usually are hoping to get to a Debt Service Coverage Ratio or DSCR of 1.25 or higher. The property is considered less risky with a higher number.

If you run your calculations and don't see that number, you too should be nervous about purchasing as the current existing income is not supporting your debt service. Which does figure your loan. How do you or the property become less risky to the bank? Putting more down payment 30 to 50% usually is sufficient. However, you have to ask yourself:

1) Do I have that?

2) How about rehab costs so I can increase the value and increase rents?
3) How about reserves for maintenance and vacancies?

Nowadays, whenever an economy is very volatile, such as we have today with the Coronavirus pandemic, banks are extremely conservative on their numbers. If you go to three different banks and they all say no, that should be a clue to perhaps stay away! It's too risky!

Banks today are looking that you have about 12 months reserves or liquidity. You don't have it? Well now you must definitely partner with someone who has potentially all the checkboxes:

1) Experience and past acquisitions
2) Liquidity and high net worth
3) Credit Worthiness not just high credit scores.

If the property is a massive undertaking, 100s of doors, and millions of dollars in price. Consider forming a *joint venture* or *syndication*.

A joint venture is more of what I just described. There's also syndication and different multiple blends or combinations on how to finance a property. Where you can have seller carry, with a JV, with a syndication.

A syndication in essence is pooling multiple people usually friends and family when you are stating out money into the acquisition of a single property. You would or should be the Managing Member of perhaps the LLC or also may be considered the General Partner or GP. Then the friends and family will buy units or shares as their participation in the property. The shares are dependent on how much they put in.

A syndication I did years ago was $25,000 per unit. Some folks did the minimum "buy in". I had some do 5 units or $125,000 invested. They may have believed or had the firepower that they were willing to invest more. Here's a pro tip. DO NOT EVER TAKE ANYONE'S MONEY ESPECIALLY IF YOU KNOW IT'S THEIR LAST FEW DOLLARS OR THE ONLY SAVINGS THEY HAVE.

Number one this is considered too risky for them. Number two talk about keeping your sanity. If you are a realtor, here is where I know you'll relate. If you ever sold a house that was $100,000 and sold another house that was $1,000,000 you may have realized in lots of cases the $100,000 home was a much harder transaction, right?

Here's often why. When people buy $1,000,000 they are much more likely "sophisticated". They are highly educated. They probably are business owners, doctors, lawyers, etc. Maybe even have other types of investments, stocks, bonds, golds, and other rentals. In investing this is actually a good thing to have a sophisticated or accredited investor.

When someone invest a lower amount of money with your syndication, beware, as I've experienced, some, not all, will be bugging you like crazy! How's the investment going? Have you started rehab? Can I come by the project? Etc.

When someone invests a larger amount of money, guess what? Since they are *sophisticated,* since they have invested before, they already know typically what to expect. You tell them we plan to have an exit strategy at year 7 or 10. They say no problem and leave you alone.

You make them really happy and exit in 5 and give them a higher return then your proforma. They start telling all their friends about their success and give you even more money! This is called "underpromise and OVERDELIVER."

That is also another pro tip. This is why you want to be really good and conservative about your numbers, not just to mitigate risk, but to reap higher returns, and make everyone happy! So you can do more and more of these!

I mentioned seller carry. There are books on this topic alone. From *subject to, lease option, AITD - all inclusive trust deed, wraparounds*, etc. I won't go much into it, but to say, the seller has maybe owned the property a long time. There's lots of equity or it's free and clear. This is where you can get really creative provided that the seller is willing to cooperate with you. The returns on this strategy could be infinite!

In financing, there's many ways to take down a property. I'd say think of your long term strategy. Being clear on this can help you have serious longevity and much success in this business.Talk to a lender, bank, or loan officer. I'd start with what kind of loans do you like doing or specialize in? Here them out, let them talk. You may find some clues on whether or not you should work with them. Remember this is a long game. This might be someone to add to your team especially if they are seasoned, knowledgeable, connected, and of course professional.

To Start Investing I Have $

_____

My F.i.c.o. / Credit Score Is:

My Top Money Friends With High Net Worth Are:

1.
2.
3.
4.
5.

CHAPTER 14 RINSE AND REPEAT - 1031 EXCHANGE

When you have a successful investment or strategy, obviously, do it again and again. If you are starting with a single family start trading your property into multiple units. Many investors will tell you if they've been at it awhile get more properties faster and bigger. Just have to ask yourself over and over, why am I doing this? Once you start to see your net worth and your cash flow increase, it almost becomes addicting in a good way. You build it up to that point where you no longer have to worry about how am I going to pay rent this month? Will I get fired this week? When will I get promoted so I can have more money and buy nicer stuff? This is freedom and refreshing!

A 1031 exchange is quite simply that. Trading up your property to like kind or better. If you have 3 single family rentals, sell them all and trade into a 10 plex or more. When you bought those, you probably bought them by yourself a few years ago the traditional way. Maybe you put 5% to 20% down. Now due to residents helping you pay them off and the appreciation in the market you can sell them for a really good down payment on a larger, better, higher performing property.

This is when you should implement the strategy. These are folks you probably need on your team as there will be lots of moving parts. If you straight up sell those 3 properties without implementing a 1031 exchange you could incur capital gains which could be a hefty amount in favor of Uncle Sam.

First make sure you talk to an "IA" Intermediary Accommodator or 1031 Exchange company. Their job is to make sure you follow strict government regulations and time frames not to trigger the capital gains. If you so touch any money or proceeds, you will forfeit any chance of having this tax benefit.

Do make sure you work with good realtors or brokers who can help you sell your properties and identify other properties on the "upleg" as sometimes, if you are getting behind on the time frames, they can help negotiate with sellers or other agents, coordinate with escrow, give the proper disclosures, stay in communication with the IA, and work in the exchange as part of your plan. Like I said, lots of moving parts.

There's definitely more to this. Just make it easy for yourself, call a 1031 exchange company and sit down with a great real estate agent if you are looking to do this. I would add that if you've partnered with anyone on these acquisitions do connect with a great attorney as well.

Is your PPM Private Placement Memorandum and Operating Agreements drawn out properly with your long game strategy? Does it have buy out clauses? What happens if you partner up with someone and they want to get out? How about if they get sued, divorced, file bankruptcy, or die? Do they want to enjoy the ride and stay in on your other future acquisitions? Should you make them a full on partner?

Yes, I am putting a little scare into this. So as you're maybe contemplating or already investing, get those wheels turning because what you don't want is a "one and done". Do one deal, screw it up so badly, lose money, and it becomes your last deal.

Just remember that there is risk in everything. You could drive to the grocery store and at no fault of your own get hit by a drunk driver. I am just saying don't let this fear stop you. You can do this with the right knowledge and right people helping you out. It becomes less risky by knowing the ins and outs of this business.

CHAPTER 15 - ACTIVE OR PASSIVE INVESTING

This chapter is in here for those that say, "I do want to invest in real estate, I think it's a great idea, I just don't want to be too involved." I've been there and done that too!

Once upon a time I read this great book on investing, sound familiar? Let me keep going, then I went to this 3 day seminar or Boot Camp. Then take it a step further, I signed up for their coaching. Here's where it got worse.

My first day of coaching, my coach asked me, "What are your plans? What are your goals?" Great starting point, right? Just like this book! Here is the kicker. I shared a few different things and then I got to the part where I said, "I want to have passive income".

This dude must have had some extra coffee or woke up on the wrong side of the bed that morning. He lit me up. "Passive, there's nothing passive in investing in multi units!" And on and on he went. In my head, I was thinking, "Are you serious? I just spent $15,000 to have you in my ear discouraging me about my plans and goals?" It was a bittersweet moment as he was actually right to an extent.

There are three ways to go about this if you want to go big and not just stick to single family homes. In a single family, you really don't need partners to some degree.

1) You could be an **Operator.**
2) You could just be an **Investor.**
3) You could be both.

The investor if they don't want to be hands on is more passive. They will invest in your deal and don't really have any say in any decision making process. There are funds, REITs, and many opportunities like this. As mentioned before, the hard part is finding or creating deals.

If you are a busy body, doctor, attorney, business owner, this may be your category. I say this with much respect. You are extremely good at your profession or you love your profession. There is nothing wrong with that at all.

The active investor is more the hands on type of person. They like going on trips to visit property. They may even like to manage people: contractors and the subs (subcontractors), other investors, lenders, tenants / residents, and property owners.

For this they may earn *acquisition fees, management fees, disposition fees*, split some of the distributions, and profit.

The passive investor will maybe get quarterly semi-annual, or yearly K-1 distributions, but again they pretty much have to sit back and be quiet.

Which sounds more like you? There are benefits and sacrifices on either or. Make sure you know who you are. Some folks are great communicators, don't actually want to be hands on, connect with other operators, and bring their fund or money partners into deals.

Yes, there's that opportunity too! If you're considering raising a fund, there's lots of things to strongly consider and be aware of too. Saying, promoting, advertising incorrectly without the right messaging and in some cases licenses, could put you in jail with potential violations of the SEC - Securities and Exchange Commission.

I throw this out again not to scare you into paralysis. Just always do the right thing, treat people right, and you'll be ok, I promise!

CHAPTER 16
SHOULD I GET A LICENSE OR NOT?

Looking back at when I was 17/18 years old, I was a scared, uneducated, inexperienced young man who lacked direction. There was no one in our family in real estate. My parents were first generation immigrants from the Philippines. Coming to the United States, they just followed directions and were without means to disrespect worker bees.

I didn't know any better. After seeing Robert Allen I was definitely sold on being an investor. However, I wasn't sold on myself. I lacked confidence in my abilities and thought getting a license and going down the path would be easier.

To some degree it was. Remember this, "the quickest way to point A to point B is a straight line." My journey in real estate had lots of turns to the left, when I should have gone right. There is no easy way to go about doing this business. It will take hard work and dedication.

You can certainly get there faster with some guidance. Do not listen to the naysayers, people who haven't been successful, that simply tried and failed. Listen to those that have made it to the top.

There will be the crabs in the bucket that will try to pull you down. Stay focused. Tell them, "thanks for sharing." Then move on. Don't let them derail you.

A license in some sense is a liability. You as a professional "should know better". I actually had a judge say that to me once. The more deals or sales you do it's not if it will happen it's when will it happen. Remember, this is America. Anyone can sue you for anything.
Align yourself with the right people and always do the right thing. When you do have a license you are obligated to disclose that. Some will love that you hold a license giving you that instant credibility.

When you don't have one, some might think you're a slime ball trying to take advantage of their situation.

This is why throughout the book I've sprinkled things on mindset and mental toughness. Every master was once a disaster. You will fail every now and then, but keep moving forward.

I know folks who will partner up. One will have a license and one won't. Even with husband and wife teams this is a common arrangement. My wife is not in the business, nor do I want her to be. I am the type of person that does want to keep it separate. It could work and lets keep it real, sometimes it won't. I've seen some couples end up in divorce because they are always "on" and don't allow time for intimacy and romance. I recommend at least once a week a "date night" if you are doing this with your significant other.

The most obvious on having a license is the commissions and referral fees. Now if you plan to go really big, I'd say have it for that, but primarily for that.

Being a real estate agent is a totally different game and more importantly mindset than being an investor. You do have to think differently about problem solving and deal structuring.

For instance, if a property is "upside down" the owner owes more to the bank than it's worth, this could be a potential short sale in which the agent may or may not get a commission. As an agent, this is what they work hardest for. There is no hourly or salary in most cases being a realtor. The only way this may be possible is if you work perhaps on a really big successful team and maybe you are a showing agent. Which in this case you'd actually be going backwards because it's really just a job.

As an investor if you happen to run across this type of scenario, you can guess multiple different ways to acquire the property: subject to, assume the loan, wholesale, etc. There are many other books out there on these topics. This is an introduction book. Those are much more advanced strategies.

Ultimately, the choice is yours. It has made me tons of money having my license. I won't complain. Would I change anything about it? Only the fact that I should have bought lots more during my career, been more fearless, and got my education way sooner on deal analysis and creative financing strategies. Other than that, no regrets.

"IF YOU CAN, YOU SHOULD, AND IF YOU'RE BRAVE ENOUGH TO START, YOU WILL."
- STEPHEN KING

CHAPTER 17 MAKE IT A MUST

I am a HUGE fan of Tony Robbins in case you haven't noticed by some of the quotes or beliefs I mention throughout the book. There's a few beliefs that I have incorporated into my mindset that definitely have helped me propel in this game of investing. Thankfully when I was in high school I do have to give credit to my mom and dad about the hustle and Tony Robbins.

As I look back and as young as I can remember, my parents did try out a few different things on the side to either build extra cash or why you're probably reading this book to eventually get financial freedom. Unfortunately, like most in America they never got to the financial freedom part.

I remember as a child growing up in Hawaii going to some random house and watching my parents learn how to put together puka shell necklaces. I am sure you'll know what these are if you've ever been there. Basically they are usually found in any store primarily as a souvenir gift from the islands. You may even get them as you exit the plane and land on islands or if you ever visit a Luau, they'll "lei you" with one of these.

After learning about how to put these puka shell necklaces together, my mom and dad got their box of supplies, went home, put them together, spent hours on their free time and weekends, and then brought them all back when dozens of them were put together. They did make a little money. I also saw that venture was short lived.

Another time I remember my mom asking me to take brochures and samples, stick them in little plastic bags, go around, and I either hung them on peoples doors, or gave them directly to people that knew me. I also remember having to take these little bags of perfume, lotions, make-up to those same people who placed orders with my mom, yes you guessed it - Avon. If you're a millennial, not sure if you know, but it's make-up and cosmetic direct distribution. It was a side hustle my mom did again to try to make money or become financially independent. Which I emphasize never happened.

Why do I bring these up? Why do I mention Tony Robbins? There was one thing my parents did do that was pretty darn impactful that I personally was able to use. One day my dad shared with me a huge box of cassette tapes. There were about 30 individual tapes. Yes, **Personal Power** by Tony Robbins.

I remember going through those tapes and doing every single exercise that was asked. One of Tony's famous beliefs is basically don't make things a should, make it a MUST. When you finish reading this book I want you to make Financial Freedom a MUST not I should do this. It's I MUST DO THIS.

My parents tried a few things and they even had a box package of a Dave Del Dotto real estate investment training program. I think it was one of their very last attempts to get to financial freedom. From that program I do remember them getting one rental. Unfortunately, they weren't fully knowledgeable, too prideful to get help, and eventually sold that investment condo. Which is a whole other story in itself.

You must make real estate investment as one of your top priorities in life. It's the only vehicle I've had that helped me accelerate my wealth, net worth, and cash flow. Even when I lost it all in 2007-2009 during the market crash. I recovered and own once again.

During the meltdown, I became very much like my parents trying many side hustles. You name it from Multi Level Marketing MLM, to Amazon drop shipping, to Shopify, etc, etc. Real estate has been the biggest and quickest way that I was able to make hundreds of thousands of dollars. None of these hustles ever got me rich or got me close to Financial Freedom.

Real estate has proven to me and many others as your very best to making lots, and lots of money. For some even financial freedom. Whether you want it now or later, START. I would also encourage you to think long term. Fixing and flipping and being a real estate agent is very short term. Yes, you could make tens of thousands and even hundreds of thousands of dollars, but guess what? You have to do it over and over again.

Buying plexes whatever asset class or niche you decide to invest in will definitely help you create a lifestyle you wish to create. Know that dollar amount you need to cover your main biggest expenses. I'd say consider what your house and car expense is. Imagine having passive income to cover those two. How much of a stress relief would that be? Will your significant other be able to stop working?

You compare it to whatever hustle you may be considering or even doing now. How many sales do you need to cover a house or car payment? Then guess what? You have to do it over and over again every month!

When you buy one rental property one time and you do your numbers right, then have a property manager help you, and his or her cost is built in, and you still are cash flowing. You only need a handful of these properties and you no longer need to hustle or work ever again.

So make this a MUST not I should do it. I MUST DO IT.

"IF YOU DON'T LIKE WHERE YOU ARE, MOVE. YOU ARE NOT A TREE."
- JIM ROHN

CHAPTER 18 THE POWER OF FOCUS

Do you really want this to work? Then it's obvious. You need to have The Power of Focus. This is your life. Life will happen. Meaning stuff, distractions, tragedies, and death may come into play in your journey, but don't let it permanently derail you.

Get back on track as quick as possible as you may lose some serious momentum that you worked so hard to obtain. You may have heard or seen a few of these that I will mention, but I want to remind you that they are the reality of your business the moment you pull away from your main objective.

Remember in science class that magnifying lens? Think of it this way. It takes a little bit to get the lens to line up with the sun just so perfectly that it makes a really bright, but small light on that piece of paper, right? That is exactly how this business is. You'll make adjustments on your scripts when talking to brokers, property managers, owners, sellers, potential hires on your team. You may not get it right the first time, but you have to keep at it to get that fire lit.

When you have that bright light on the paper that's perfectly aligned with the sun and the paper, hold it there long enough, that smoke will start to show and then eureka, you've got fire! Just like your business. You may be sending letters to potential owners, absentees, probates, notice of defaults, expireds, for sale by owners, divorces, etc. if some of these went over your head, *just Google it.*

Those by the way are ones I would recommend to target market if you want even bigger steeper discounts and deals!

Hopefully, you're understanding why it is imperative to focus. I am NOT saying if something happens that is tragic to ignore it, do take the time to mourn, settle out formalities, whatever. Oftentimes, keeping very, very busy is really good for you because sitting still feeling sorry for yourself, feeling like you're the victim of whatever happened or is happening is way more destructible than putting that focus energy, and rechannelling that fuel back into your mission.

Another example I can share is from one of the other greats Zig Ziglar. I remember I was at a sales training and watched this VHS tape. Yes, I said it. Kids, if that went over your head, GTS. So back to Zig. I was watching Zig and he gave an example of focus and momentum.

You may or may not relate. If you go to Knott's Berry Farm in California, travel to more rural areas of the US or other countries, (I remembered seeing this in the Philippines) in order to get water, you have to pump it out of the ground. Now visualize this. If the pump hasn't been used for a period of time the water is way deeper in the ground.

In order to get the water into your bucket, you must "prime the pump". In other words, take that handle and start this up and down motion, DON'T STOP, and don't let go of the handle. You must pump, and pump, and pump some more, until you see some water coming out.

This is the same for this business. Whether you use a broker, do this solo, with a partner, or team, no matter what you must have serious focus.

Sending out letters, door knocking, searching Loopnet, Zillow, Craigslist, making offers, sending out LOIs, etc The moment you stop or let go of that handle, you lose all that moment you created and that water goes back into the ground.

Now with that pump, the water will come out slowly at first. It doesn't mean you stop marketing. You keep pumping until the water is gushing out like a mini Niagara Falls. Then guess what? Don't let go! Have someone else get on that handle and keep pumping up and down or build a machine that will pump it automatically for you.

In other words, people and a system. Yes, that's how you can even scale from one building or unit to tens of hundreds of doors or buildings! You want to go really big? FOCUS.

Do not stop. Keep going until you've hit your goal. This works on anything and any business.

How bad do you want it? Then FOCUS.

"THE DIFFERENCE BETWEEN A SUCCESSFUL PERSON AND OTHERS IS NOT A LACK OF STRENGTH, NOT A LACK OF KNOWLEDGE, BUT RATHER A LACK OF WILL." - VINCE LOMBARDI

CHAPTER 19
FOLLOW A FORMULA

Why reinvent the wheel they say, right? What is tried and true? Still unclear? Try this on for size. My good friend Hector shared this simple rule with me **"4/3/1"**. Hector is a simple guy with extraordinary talent and focus. He mentioned to me one day on making money and growing wealth: Buy 4, Flip 3, Keep 1. When you don't have a lot of money or reserves, stack that cash!

This is a very simple formula. Need cash before investing for the long haul? Buy 4 flips and either wholesale them out to other flippers or take them down as a flip of your own and then stockpile that money. Only keep the winners if you see some could realize really great NET cash flow, demand is extremely high like it's near a really great school, or in the path of progress. You could get really lucky once in a while and hit a home run.

For instance in raw land. A farmer may see it for great dirt for his crops and pay $100,000. A developer may see that huge companies are coming in like Tesla, Amazon, etc and realize that it may be wise to pay a higher premium if need be because it will be worth way more when something like this happens. This unfortunately, falls into more the speculation investing, so please be careful on this! I bought several rental properties where there was even negative cash flow. I flipped some of them at the right time and did great on the sale. When the market suddenly turns or something happens locally like a major business shuts down, this could be disastrous!

Knowing your numbers, jobs, population increasing or decreasing, market rent, local news, trends, applications for permits, tenant or landlord favorability, and of course location, location, location is crucial to these formulas. Don't just rely on google maps. Have "boots on the ground". People that you really know, like and trust who can help you.

Don't keep properties that you might be having trouble renting out upon them being vacant. For example, one bedroom usually will take longer to rent out than 2 and 3 bedrooms. Houses next to schools are pretty attractive just as long as it's not on the main road of the school (high traffic and walkers before and after school is a high liability). Need some more help? Ask a great realtor or other investors for more information and diligently study these areas very carefully.

Here's another formula that might be also simple. Andrew Holmes, a friend of mine in the Chicago area who runs several Real Estate Investment Clubs shared his formula of **"2/5/7"**. In 2 years buy 5 homes and pay them all off in seven. This formula usually works better in the midwest where the prices of homes are a lot lower and the rents collected are sufficient to cover the debt service when compared to places like San Diego, Seattle, San Francisco, etc.

This also works very well for the busy professionals making significant income that have the ability to put 20% down or more. When you put this much down and ARE NOT cash flowing DO NOT buy that house. Seriously, what's the advantage? What's your goal? Look for another property or marketplace where you get a better ROI or return on investment.

In addition to this strategy, you'll use the extra cash flow to add towards principal pay down. It's suggested that any surplus monies you earn double up payments and accelerate paying your rentals off quickly. If you're in sales and earn commissions for a living, any big months and bonuses, make the sacrifices now and pay off your loans quickly.

Again, this depends on your strategy and maybe even your age. When you're still single and don't have kids, your expenses are usually lower than someone who's married and with kids. Be FRUGAL. Live today how others won't to live tomorrow how others can't or never will!

You've probably also heard of the "BRRR Strategy", right? No? Here it is in a nutshell. Buy. Rehab. Rent. Refinance. Repeat. If you've put together all the bits and pieces to this puzzle you'll eventually end up here or in a few variations of the aforementioned.

Buy a fixer. Something that you could get ideally 30-50% below market value. ***Rehab*** the property, fix it up, add value, and make it more attractive. Next, ***Rent*** the property out. Then ***Refinance*** - pull your original cash out. You may have used hard money or a private lender to acquire. At which point the interest rates are probably extremely pretty high. This should be a definite no brainer to refinance. Remember, you don't get wealthy selling real estate like an agent or wholesaler. You get wealthy buying and keeping your purchases! Lastly, **Repeat** the process.

As Dan Pena may say, you know what, "JFDI - Just F'ing Do It!"

CONCLUSION

In summary, what is a Plex? A plex in my mind is more than one. It could be several single family homes, multiple-doors (even a single unit renting out several rooms - like house hacking or bigger multiple apartment buildings), multiple-retail/office tenants, or any other type of multi-plex your creative genius can think of. Robert Kiyosaki said it best in **Rich Dad Poor Dad.** Your house that you own and live in is a liability. Any other types of real estate you invest in that creates cash flow is an asset. If you do it right, the more the merrier. However, remember, **Begin With The End In Mind.**

Some folks I've interviewed over the years in acquisition have this grandiose idea of owning 100s of 1000s of doors. Most I've noticed it's either a fun game to them or on the flip side some make that claim early in their career simply to edify their ego. To some degree it's a good idea, but to some it's definitely not. It's one of those things like the late rapper Biggie Smalls once said, "More money, more problems." I'd say yes and no.

If you don't know how to properly manage money, then yes it's a problem. If you don't know how to manage people who help you manage your money or assets, yes it's a problem. If you don't know how to build or create systems in this business to manage your rental income money, read the proformas, rent rolls, spreadsheets, then yes, it could be a serious problem.

However, if you know that end goal what you're going for or lifestyle you're looking to create, surround yourself with the right people, read the applicable books on mindset and real estate, continue to stay razor sharp on trends, marketplaces, consumer demands, live to give, and help others, you will have the most incredible life even more than you've probably imagined!

How do I know? I've personally coached and mentored hundreds of people who have achieved that. I've been surrounded by people and interviewed people that actually have done it as well. Is it real? Is it possible?

You bet it is! Like Napoleon Hill says in **Think and Grow Rich,** "Whatever the mind can conceive and believe, it can achieve.

I wish you all the best in your journey. I hope that you took away at least one golden nugget or two.

If not, please do me the honor and share this book with someone that you think that may benefit from it. I'm so grateful that my Uncle shared that seminar with Robert Allen when I was a teenager in high school. That small gesture changed my life forever.

This book may have been somewhat basic for some or hopefully gave more juice for those already inspired. I am just putting it out there in hopes to inspire others and share.

Pay it forward. Whatever goes around, comes around. Take care and God bless.

RESOURCES

I firmly believe that you can make any business scalable in (2) ways: 1) People and 2) Systems. These tools and resources are provided to help you scale and perhaps automate your investing business. I have either used these companies or tools myself or have had my clients and friends use them. Many of these recommendations do have FREE trials. Sometimes I may find a better tool or resource same with you. That is partly why we don't necessarily promote specific company domains as sometimes our research may suggest something else that's better. Try them out, if you don't like them, cancel and try something else. Make progress by continuously moving forward.

1) If you have a regular day job, someone else should be answering your phones. You cannot afford to lose any leads while at your day job. **http://myvahack.com/**

2) Do you want to source deals yourself? In some cases you should, think of bypassing a broker and dealing directly with the owner. **http://www.findhiddendeals.com/**

3) Having trouble with your calculations? Is excel too basic or insufficient? **http://bestdarncalculator.com/**

4) Ready to do some cold calling? Can't find the numbers in your farm? (Know the laws. Use your discre-

tion) **http://ineedphonenumbers.com/**

5) How are you going to follow up and stay in touch with your leads, investors, or build your database? Should you create a customized email drip? **http://bestemailcompany.com/**

6) Are you ready to get into real estate as a realtor or looking for a new company? **http://becomearealpro.com/**

7) Do you need a coach or some consulting? Do you need more ideas and accountability? Are you looking to go deeper on these ideas and strategies? **https://www.coachjoemendoza.com/**

8) Want to learn more about real estate and investing or seeking some additional entertainment? **Watch or listen online to:** *The Real Estate Raw Show*

DISCLAIMER:

Techniques, suggestions, and mentions referenced in this book, The Real Estate Raw Show, The Joe Mendoza Show, blog posts, or social media posts are the opinion of Joe Mendoza or associates. Readers and listeners are encouraged to do their own research and due diligence implementing any ideas that were shared. Some of these recommendations are affiliate links, which means that if you click on one of the product links, Joe Mendoza or Joe Mendoza Team, Inc may potentially receive compensation. This helps support the marketing and promotion of this book and other messaging efforts that the team and Joe Mendoza are working on. It also allows us to continue to bring more enriching concepts, ideas, and tools to you. Reliance on any of these methods in this book, on our shows, or even at our events to be used at your discretion. Joe Mendoza, Joe Mendoza Team, Inc., and it's owners, affiliates, officers, agents, and employees will not be held liable for any damages, losses, or liabilities, including causes of action of any nature whatsoever arising out of usage of the information shared in this book, our shows, posts, blogs, or any of our events.

ABOUT THE AUTHOR

Joe Mendoza has been involved in real estate and business for nearly 30 years. He is an active Investor, Real Estate Broker, highly sought out Speaker, and Worldwide Business Coach.

He has personally owned, represented clientele, and helped manage multiplexes. Joe has also other experiences such as participating in several different development and redevelopment projects including a 60 unit condo conversion in Las Vegas, Nevada, a 17 unit office building in Escondido, California, a 10 unit condo conversion in El Cajon, CA; a 4 plex in Escondido California, a raw land development in Spring Valley, CA; and multiple "fix and flips".

Mr. Mendoza has a long track record of success. 100's of millions of dollars of real estate transactions. Hundreds of people mentored, coached, and trained. He's been a guest several times on local news and radio to advise on the real estate market. Also recognizing his efforts, various publications have featured Mr. Mendoza in the San Diego Union Tribune, the Wall Street Journal, the Real Estate Book, the Asian Journal, the Harmon Homes Magazine, and other similar publications. While at Prudential California Realty, he ranked as high as the Top 1% in the nation, and was number 7 in all of Southern California.

He holds a Bachelors of Arts degree from San Diego State University and has a high passion for contribution volunteering where needed in multiple activities that either of his two children participates in from Boy Scouts of America to various sports and has sat on multiple non-profit Board of Directors.

Are you looking for a trusted advisor in business or real estate? Perhaps help to get to the next level in business or life? Joe is the MAN!

JOE MENDOZA

PO Box 188
San Marcos, CA 92079
Toll-Free (877) 794-5227
www.JoeMendoza.com

Thank you for the continued support!

www.ingramcontent.com/pod-product-compliance
Lightning Source LLC
Chambersburg PA
CBHW071423210526
45465CB00001B/497